GREATEST OF ALL TIME
SPORTS STARS

THE GREATEST
BASKETBALL PLAYERS
OF ALL TIME

Gareth Stevens
PUBLISHING

BY MATTHEW JANKOWSKI

Please visit our website, www.garethstevens.com. For a free color catalog of all our high-quality books, call toll free 1-800-542-2595 or fax 1-877-542-2596.

Cataloging-in-Publication Data

Names: Jankowski, Matthew.
Title: The greatest basketball players of all time / Matthew Jankowski.
Description: New York : Gareth Stevens Publishing, 2020. | Series: Greatest of all time: sports stars | Includes glossary and index.
Identifiers: ISBN 9781538247754 (pbk.) | ISBN 9781538247778 (library bound) | ISBN 9781538247761 (6 pack)
Subjects: LCSH: Basketball players–United States–Biography–Juvenile literature. | Basketball–United States–History–Juvenile literature.
Classification: LCC GV885.1 J36 2019 | DDC 796.323 B–dc23

First Edition

Published in 2020 by
Gareth Stevens Publishing
111 East 14th Street, Suite 349
New York, NY 10003

Designer: Katelyn E. Reynolds
Editor: Emily Mahoney

Photo credits: Cover, p. 1 Jonathan Bachman/Getty Images; cover, pp. 1–32 (series art) Dmitry Kostrov/Shutterstock.com; cover, pp. 1–32 (series background) rangizzz/Shutterstock.com; p. 5 Martin Good/Shutterstock.com; pp. 6, 22 Bettmann/Getty Images; pp. 7, 29 (basketball graphic) Timothy W. Stone/Shutterstock.com; pp. 9, 11, 15, 24, 25 Focus on Sport/Getty Images; p. 10 BRIAN BAHR/AFP/Getty Images; p. 12 Jed Jacobsohn/Getty Images; p. 13 MATT CAMPBELL/AFP/Getty Images; p. 16 Jason Miller/Getty Images; pp. 17, 28 Christian Petersen/Getty Images; p. 18 GEORGE FREY/AFP/Getty Images; p. 19 Norm Purdue/NBAE via Getty Images; p. 21 Stephen Dunn/Getty Images; p. 23 Paul Natkin/Getty Images; p. 26 Lisa Blumenfeld/Getty Images; p. 27 Lisa Blumenfeld/NBAE/Getty Images.

CPSIA compliance information: Batch #CW20GS: For further information contact Gareth Stevens, New York, New York at 1-800-542-2595.

CONTENTS

WORDS IN THE GLOSSARY APPEAR IN **BOLD** TEXT THE FIRST TIME THEY ARE USED IN THE TEXT.

FIRST STEP ONTO THE COURT

In 1891, James Naismith, a gym class instructor of Springfield College in Massachusetts, grabbed two peach baskets, hung them on the walls of a gymnasium and had students try to put a ball into the basket. And just like that, the first ever game of basketball was played!

Basketball grew in popularity until the National Basketball Association (NBA) was formed in 1946. From that point forward, basketball was no longer just a game, but a professional sport with teams and a league. In this book, you'll learn about the greatest basketball players to ever compete and exactly what made them the best of the best.

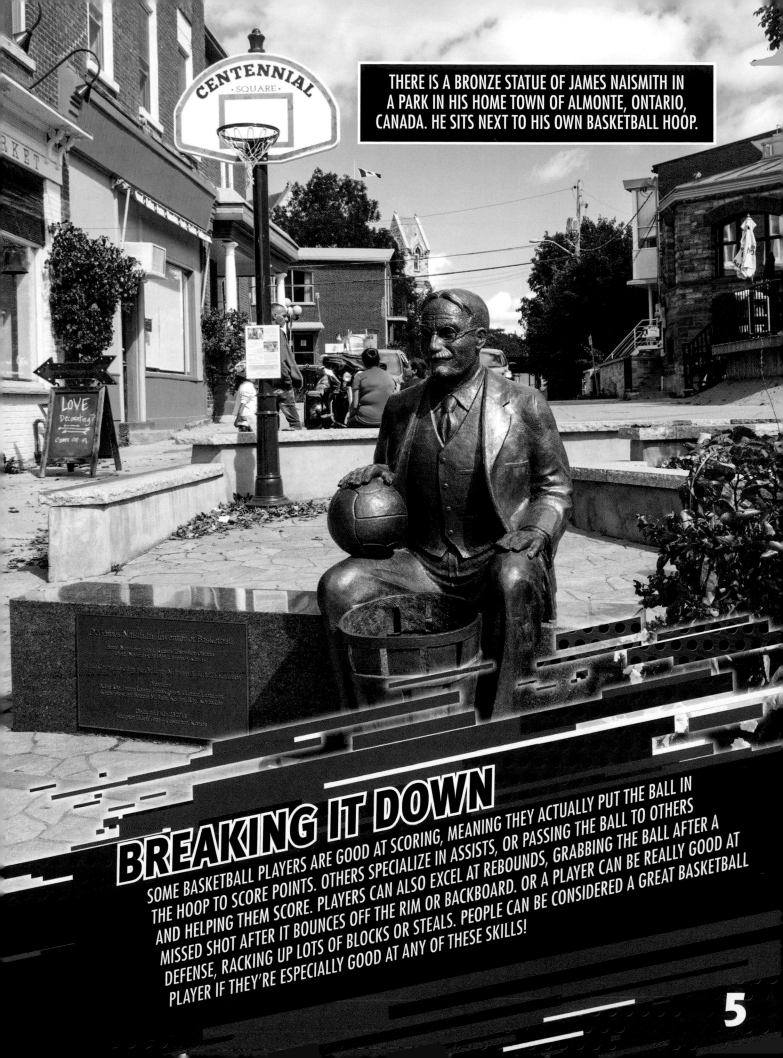

THERE IS A BRONZE STATUE OF JAMES NAISMITH IN A PARK IN HIS HOME TOWN OF ALMONTE, ONTARIO, CANADA. HE SITS NEXT TO HIS OWN BASKETBALL HOOP.

BREAKING IT DOWN

SOME BASKETBALL PLAYERS ARE GOOD AT SCORING, MEANING THEY ACTUALLY PUT THE BALL IN THE HOOP TO SCORE POINTS. OTHERS SPECIALIZE IN ASSISTS, OR PASSING THE BALL TO OTHERS AND HELPING THEM SCORE. PLAYERS CAN ALSO EXCEL AT REBOUNDS, GRABBING THE BALL AFTER A MISSED SHOT AFTER IT BOUNCES OFF THE RIM OR BACKBOARD. OR A PLAYER CAN BE REALLY GOOD AT DEFENSE, RACKING UP LOTS OF BLOCKS OR STEALS. PEOPLE CAN BE CONSIDERED A GREAT BASKETBALL PLAYER IF THEY'RE ESPECIALLY GOOD AT ANY OF THESE SKILLS!

POINT GUARDS:
BOB "THE COOZ" COUSY

The year was 1950. The NBA, just 4 years old, was ready for a player to make the game his own. After being benched in college because his coach didn't like his **revolutionary** style, Bob "the Cooz" Cousy **prevailed** over his difficulties to become an all-time great. If you liked behind-the-back passes and no-look dump offs, then Cousy was your man.

Known for assisting his teammates to victory, Bob Cousy won six NBA championships and played in 13 straight NBA All-Star games. He led the league in assists for eight seasons in a row and in 1970 was elected into the Basketball Hall of Fame.

COUSY WAS PART OF THE 1959-1960 BOSTON CELTICS THAT IS WIDELY REGARDED AS ONE OF THE GREATEST BASKETBALL TEAMS OF ALL TIME.

GREATEST TEAMS OF ALL-TIME
ACCORDING TO ESPN

TEAM	STARTING LINEUP	WHAT MAKES THEM GREAT?
1. 1959-60 BOSTON CELTICS	PG BOB COUSY SG BILL SHARMAN SF FRANK RAMSEY PF TOM HEINSOHN C BILL RUSSELL	**REGULAR SEASON** 59 WINS, 16 LOSSES **WON NATIONAL CHAMPIONSHIP** 8 WINS, 5 LOSSES IN PLAYOFFS
2. 2017-18 GOLDEN STATE WARRIORS	PG STEPHEN CURRY SG KLAY THOMPSON SF KEVIN DURANT PF DRAYMOND GREEN C ZAZA PACHULIA	**REGULAR SEASON** 58 WINS, 24 LOSSES **WON NATIONAL CHAMPIONSHIP** 16 WINS, 5 LOSSES IN PLAYOFFS
3. 2015-16 CLEVELAND CAVALIERS	PG KYRIE IRVING SG J. R. SMITH SF LEBRON JAMES PF TRISTAN THOMPSON C KEVIN LOVE	**REGULAR SEASON** 57 WINS, 25 LOSSES **WON NATIONAL CHAMPIONSHIP** 16 WINS, 5 LOSSES IN PLAYOFFS
4. 2000-01 LOS ANGELES LAKERS	PG DEREK FISHER SG KOBE BRYANT SF RICK FOX PF HORACE GRANT C SHAQUILLE O'NEAL	**REGULAR SEASON** 56 WINS, 26 LOSSES **WON NATIONAL CHAMPIONSHIP** 15 WINS, 1 LOSS IN PLAYOFFS
5. 2014-15 GOLDEN STATE WARRIORS	PG STEPHEN CURRY SG KLAY THOMPSON SF HARRISON BARNES PF DRAYMOND GREEN C ANDREW BOGUT	**REGULAR SEASON** 67 WINS, 15 LOSSES **WON NATIONAL CHAMPIONSHIP** 16 WINS, 5 LOSSES IN PLAYOFFS

POINT GUARDS

BOB COUSY PLAYED AT THE POINT GUARD POSITION. POINT GUARDS ARE THE PLAYMAKERS ON THE COURT. OFTEN THE SHORTEST AND MOST **AGILE** PLAYERS, POINT GUARDS LOOK TO ADVANCE THE BALL, READ THE DEFENSE AND SET THEIR TEAMMATES UP TO SCORE. "THE COOZ" EXCELLED AS A POINT GUARD WITH HIS CREATIVITY AND FAST PASSES.

POINT GUARDS: EARVIN "MAGIC" JOHNSON

Imagine being so good at basketball that everyone simply called you "Magic." Earvin "Magic" Johnson played point guard for 13 seasons for the Los Angeles Lakers in the 1980s. Magic dazzled fans with a joyful energy and passion for the game. He spun defenders in circles with his passing skills.

Magic made the basketball term **"triple-double"** popular, as he could pass, score, and grab rebounds for an amazing all-around game. He could even play lockdown defense. Magic won five championships, was named Most Valuable Player (MVP) three times, and was selected 12 times as an All-Star. When he **retired** from basketball, he had the all-time record for most assists.

A TRUE LEGEND

MAGIC JOHNSON HAD A **RIVALRY** WITH ANOTHER OF THE GREATEST BASKETBALL PLAYERS OF ALL TIME: LARRY BIRD. THE TWO FACED EACH OTHER IN COLLEGE IN THE 1979 NCAA CHAMPIONSHIP GAME (WHICH MAGIC WON). THEY THEN WENT ON TO COMPETE IN THE NBA FINALS THREE TIMES IN THE 1980S (MAGIC WON TWO OF THEM). THE TWO PLAYERS RESPECTED EACH OTHER. BIRD SAID: "MAGIC IS HEAD AND SHOULDERS ABOVE EVERYBODY ELSE. I'VE NEVER SEEN (ANYBODY) AS GOOD AS HIM."

SHOOTING GUARDS: MICHAEL "MJ" JORDAN

Michael Jordan is considered by many to be the greatest player ever to step on the court. He was MVP five times, won the NBA championship six times, and was the highest scoring player for 10 seasons. Often called by his initials "MJ," Michael was electrifying for fans to watch.

MJ was known for his **determination**. Once he got in the zone, he could be seen sticking his tongue out while driving to the hoop and throwing down one of his famous "Air Jordan" acrobatic dunks. Jordan's game has also been described as clutch since he scored many buzzer-beater shots to win games.

AIR JORDANS

ALONG WITH BASKETBALL GREATNESS, MJ IS KNOWN FOR HIS FAMOUS "JORDAN" LINE OF FOOTWEAR. YOU MAY HAVE SEEN BASKETBALL SHOES OR SANDALS FEATURING HIS "AIR JORDAN" POSE. BASKETBALL SHOES OFFER ANKLE SUPPORT BECAUSE PLAYERS MOVE QUICKLY ON THE COURT. EVEN AFTER RETIRING, MJ INSPIRES PLAYERS TO KEEP DUNKING EVERY DAY.

SHOOTING GUARDS: KOBE BRYANT

Scoring baskets is what Kobe Bryant did best, so the position of shooting guard was a good fit. He **swished** so many shots by taking a fadeaway jumper, the shot became known as a "Kobe" on playground basketball courts. Kobe was so good that he started playing in the NBA right after he finished high school!

Kobe played his whole 20-year career for the Los Angeles Lakers. He has scored the third most points of all-time and during one game, he managed to score 81 points all on his own! Kobe won five championships, two Olympic gold medals, and was selected as an All-Star 17 times.

FROM 1996 TO 2016, KOBE FILLED HIGHLIGHT REELS WHILE WEARING THE **ICONIC** PURPLE AND YELLOW COLORS OF THE LAKERS

KOBE AND SHAQ

THE LOS ANGELES LAKERS WERE A POWERHOUSE IN THE NBA FROM 2002 TO 2004. KOBE WAS PART OF A FEARED DYNAMIC DUO ALONG WITH THE "BIG DADDY" SHAQUILLE O'NEAL PLAYING CENTER. TOGETHER THEY WON THREE CHAMPIONSHIPS IN A ROW!

SMALL FORWARDS: LARRY BIRD

The best word to describe Larry Bird's style of basketball is hustle! With every play of every game and even every practice, Larry could be seen giving it his all. Offense or defense, he never took a play off. Larry's hard work made him a steady athlete and **dependable** teammate.

Larry Bird was drafted by the Boston Celtics and played there for his whole 13-year career. Larry was such a good shooter, he sometimes practiced taking three-pointers with his eyes closed. Larry Bird won three championships, and was the league MVP 3 years in a row.

LARRY BIRD PROVED THAT PRACTICE MAKES PERFECT. HE HOLDS THE THIRD LONGEST FREE THROW STREAK IN HISTORY, MAKING 71 FREE THROWS IN A ROW!

ANOTHER PATH TO GREATNESS

LARRY BIRD HAD SO MUCH PASSION FOR BASKETBALL THAT HE DIDN'T LET CAREER-ENDING INJURIES TAKE HIM AWAY FROM THE SPORT. INSTEAD, HE DECIDED TO COACH FOR 3 YEARS FOR THE INDIANA PACERS. DURING HIS FIRST COACHING SEASON, HE WON THE NBA COACH OF THE YEAR AWARD, SHOWING THAT HE PUT HIS BASKETBALL SMARTS TO GOOD USE.

15

SMALL FORWARDS: LEBRON "KING JAMES" JAMES

They call him "the king" for a reason. LeBron James might be the most complete basketball player ever. He went to the NBA straight from high school and in only 3 years, he turned the Cleveland Cavaliers from the worst team in the league to championship contenders.

King James is a four-time MVP, has won three championships, and has already scored the fourth-most points in NBA history. Because he is so dangerous, LeBron often draws two or more defenders to try to stop him. A quick pass sets up his teammates to hit open shots.

LEBRON JAMES IS A TRUE FORCE ON THE COURT. HE HAS THE SIZE AND SPEED TO DRIVE TO THE HOOP, HIT THREE-POINTERS, AND MUSCLE OUT THE OPPONENT TO GRAB REBOUNDS.

CONTINUING GREATNESS

YOU CAN WATCH KING JAMES LIGHT UP THE COURT RIGHT NOW. LEBRON WON CHAMPIONSHIPS WITH THE CLEVELAND CAVALIERS AND THE MIAMI HEAT, AND HE JOINED THE LOS ANGELES LAKERS IN 2018. AS LONG AS HE STAYS HEALTHY, THERE ARE NO SIGNS THAT HE WILL RETIRE SOON!

POWER FORWARDS:
KARL "THE MAILMAN" MALONE

Did someone order a special delivery? Karl "the Mailman" Malone knew all about shipping the basketball right through the hoop. Malone has the second-most points scored of any player in NBA history. He played for 18 seasons altogether, with 17 of those on the Utah Jazz.

The Mailman was the perfect combination of size and straight-up shooting. He could muscle his way to dunk in the face of a defender or step back and hit a jump shot. The Mailman and his teammate John Stockton terrified the league with their pick-and-roll plays.

KARL MALONE WOULD SET A PICK BY STANDING IN THE WAY OF A DEFENDER AND THEN ROLL OFF TO RECEIVE A PASS TOWARD THE BASKET. THAT'S WHY THEY CALL IT A PICK-AND-ROLL PLAY.

KAR MALONE WAS NICKNAMED "THE MAILMAN" BECAUSE HE ALWAYS DELIVERED! HERE HE CAN BE SEEN SLAM DUNKING FOR THE UTAH JAZZ.

TOUGH LUCK

THERE IS ONE UNIQUE FACT THAT SETS KARL MALONE APART FROM ALL OF THE OTHER ATHLETES IN THIS BOOK. FOR EVERY SINGLE SEASON MALONE PLAYED FOR THE UTAH JAZZ, THEY MADE IT TO THE PLAYOFFS, BUT OVER 18 YEARS, THEY NEVER ACTUALLY WON A SINGLE CHAMPIONSHIP! THEY MADE THE FINALS TWICE IN A ROW, BUT BOTH TIMES, THEY LOST TO MICHAEL JORDAN'S CHICAGO BULLS. BAD LUCK RUNNING INTO MJ TWICE!

POWER FORWARDS:
TIM "THE BIG FUNDAMENTAL" DUNCAN

Tim "The Big Fundamental" Duncan reminded the NBA that teams win by scoring the most points, not by how they score them. Duncan played his entire career for the San Antonio Spurs and while he did, the Spurs won over 50 games for 17 straight seasons. That's the longest streak in NBA history!

Tim Duncan was famous for bank shots, using the backboard to make sure his shots went in. The Big Fundamental also showed his defensive **prowess**, clearing the opponent's misses with his rebounds and blocking their lay ups. Tim Duncan won five championships and is the only player with over 1000 wins with one team!

TIM DUNCAN PLAYED SOLID BASKETBALL, LEADING TO THE NICKNAME "THE BIG FUNDAMENTAL." HE WASN'T SUPER FLASHY ABOUT IT, BUT HE GOT THE JOB DONE.

THE FIRST CHOICE

TIM DUNCAN WAS THE FIRST PLAYER DRAFTED OVERALL IN THE 1997 NBA DRAFT. DRAFTING IS WHEN PROFESSIONAL SPORTS TEAMS SELECT PLAYERS WHO ARE LEAVING COLLEGE TO PLAY FOR THEIR TEAM. OTHER FIRST OVERALL DRAFT PICKS FROM THIS BOOK INCLUDE: MAGIC JOHNSON, LEBRON JAMES, KAREEM ABDUL-JABBAR, AND DIANA TAURASI.

CENTERS:
WILT "THE BIG DIPPER" CHAMBERLAIN

Wilt Chamberlain was a superstar who played during the 1960s. Wilt scored, and he scored a lot. He is the only player to score over 4,000 points in one season! To prove he wasn't selfish either, Wilt also had one season with the most assists in the league.

Wilt was so good at scoring that opponents would have two or sometimes three defenders guard him. They would even **foul** him on purpose so he didn't have a chance to shoot. "The Big Dipper" was **unfazed**, however. He is the only player to score 100 points in a single game.

ROCKIN' REBOUNDS

A REBOUND IS WHEN A PLAYER GRABS THE BALL AFTER A MISSED SHOT. WILT CHAMBERLAIN HOLDS THE RECORD FOR MOST REBOUNDS OF ALL-TIME WITH OVER 23,000. HE ALSO HAS THE MOST REBOUNDS IN A SINGLE GAME WITH 55. WHEN "THE BIG DIPPER" WANTED THE BALL, GOOD LUCK TRYING TO STOP HIM!

CENTERS:
KAREEM ABDUL-JABBAR

Similar to Wilt Chamberlain, Kareem Abdul-Jabbar was super talented at scoring. Kareem has the most career points scored of any NBA player in history! The real thing that sets him apart from the other players in this book however, is Kareem's sportsmanship.

Kareem Abdul-Jabbar was originally named Ferdinand Alcindor Jr., but changed his name after he began practicing the Islamic faith. Kareem played according to his religious beliefs. He watched hours of game film, meditated prior to games and remained **disciplined** on the court. He gave his team a quiet confidence, and showed his teammates that games could be won through continued practice and staying mentally strong.

KAREEM ABDUL-JABBAR IS KNOWN FOR HIS ICONIC "SKY HOOK" SHOT, WHERE HE TOSSES THE BALL UP OVER THE SIDE OF HIS HEAD.

MANY AWARDS

KAREEM WAS INDUCTED INTO THE NBA HALL OF FAME IN 1995. BY THE TIME HE RETIRED, HE HAD WON THE ROOKIE OF THE YEAR AWARD, WAS ON SIX TEAMS WHO WON THE NBA CHAMPIONSHIP, AND WAS THE LEAGUE MVP SIX TIMES. KAREEM PLAYED FOR 20 YEARS AND DID NOT STOP UNTIL HE WAS 42 YEARS OLD.

CENTER: LISA "SMOOTH" LESLIE

In 1996, women changed basketball forever with the creation of the Women's National Basketball Association, or WNBA. Lisa "Smooth" Leslie was at the first conference where the WNBA was officially approved by the Board of Governors. She didn't waste any time taking over the league.

At 6 feet, 5 inches (1.96 m) tall, Lisa took charge under the hoop when she played the center position. "Smooth" led the Los Angeles Sparks to two WNBA championships and also won the league MVP three times. She became the first WNBA player to win the best player award during the season, playoffs, and All-Star game!

LISA LESLIE SPARKED EXCITEMENT FOR FANS WHEN SHE WAS THE FIRST WOMAN TO SLAM DUNK IN A PROFESSIONAL BASKETBALL GAME.

GREATNESS ON AND OFF THE COURT

LISA LESLIE STOOD AS AN EXAMPLE OF A WOMAN WHO DID JUST WHAT SHE WANTED. AFTER PLAYING 10 YEARS IN THE WNBA, SHE SAT OUT OF THE 2007 SEASON BECAUSE SHE WAS PREGNANT WITH HER DAUGHTER. SHE CAME RIGHT BACK IN THE 2008 SEASON, BALANCING **ASPIRATIONS** OF BEING BOTH A PROFESSIONAL ATHLETE AND A MOTHER.

27

SHOOTING GUARD: DIANA "WHITE MAMBA" TAURASI

No list of greatest WNBA players would be complete without Diana Taurasi. She was nicknamed "White Mamba" by Kobe Bryant, since he was impressed by how deadly she was on the court. As the first pick of the WNBA draft in 2004, Taurasi was expected to be great. And she delivered, winning Rookie of the Year that season.

White Mamba holds the record for the most points scored in a single season with 860. Diana also owns the all-time record for most three-point shots in WNBA history with 1,102. And the number will only go up as she keeps playing!

THE FIVE GREATEST TEAMS IN WNBA HISTORY

TEAM	WHAT MADE THEM THE BEST
HOUSTON COMETS	THE COMETS WON THE FIRST FOUR CHAMPIONSHIPS IN WNBA HISTORY!
LOS ANGELES SPARKS	THE SPARKS DEFEATED THE COMETS WITH STELLAR PLAY BY LISA LESLIE TO WIN THREE CHAMPIONSHIPS OVERALL.
DETROIT SHOCK	THE SHOCK HAVE WON THREE WNBA CHAMPIONSHIPS AND ARE THE FIRST TEAM TO GO FROM WORST IN THE LEAGUE TO CHAMPIONS THE NEXT SEASON!
PHOENIX MERCURY	DIANA TAURASI PLAYED FOR THIS TEAM. THE MERCURY HAVE WON THREE CHAMPIONSHIPS OVERALL.
MINNESOTA LYNX	THE LYNX WON TWO CHAMPIONSHIPS IN THREE SEASONS AND LOOK TO ONLY BE GETTING BETTER. WATCH OUT!

OLYMPIC GREATNESS

GREAT PLAYERS DON'T JUST SHINE IN THE NBA AND WNBA. EVERY 4 YEARS, THE WORLD'S BEST PLAYERS COMPETE IN THE SUMMER OLYMPICS. DIANA TAURASI AND LISA LESLIE HAVE BOTH WON FOUR GOLD MEDALS AT THE OLYMPICS. MEANWHILE, THE US MEN'S TEAM HAS WON THE OLYMPIC TOURNAMENT 15 OUT OF 19 TIMES. THIS INCLUDES THE FAMOUS 1992 DREAM TEAM, WHICH FEATURED FOUR OF THE GREATS FROM THIS BOOK: MICHAEL JORDAN, LARRY BIRD, MAGIC JOHNSON, AND KARL MALONE.

GLOSSARY

agile: able to move quickly and easily

aspirations: something that a person wants very much to achieve

dependable: able to be trusted to do what is needed

determination: the act of deciding something firmly

discipline: a kind of training

foul: an action against the rules for which a player gets a penalty

iconic: a person who is very successful and admired

prevail: to defeat an opponent in a long or difficult contest

prowess: great ability or skill

retire: to leave a job at the end of a career

revolutionary: causing a great or complete change

rivalry: when two teams compete with each other often

swished: sink a shot without the ball touching the backboard or rim

triple-double: the achievement of a player who gets 10 or more points, assists and rebounds in one game

unfazed: not confused, worried, or shocked by something that has happened

FOR MORE INFORMATION

BOOKS

Bryant, Howard. *Legends: The Best Players, Games, and Teams in Basketball.* London, United Kingdom: Puffin Books, 2017.

Levit, Joseph. *Basketball's G.O.A.T.: Michael Jordan, LeBron James, and More.* Minneapolis, MN: Lerner Publications, 2020.

Walters, John. *Top 10 Basketball Superstars.* Mankato, MN: Child's World, 2019.

WEBSITES

Basketball: Learn All About the Sport Basketball
www.ducksters.com/sports/basketball.php
Check out this educational website that contains games and links to learn more about all of the ins and outs of the game!

Jr. NBA
www.jr.nba.com/
Find out more about youth basketball leagues and read practice plans that kids can use to develop their own skills on the court!

The Official Site of the NBA
www.nba.com
Read up on NBA stats, standings and player biographies. The site also contains video clips and highlights!

INDEX